CRATHIE Parish Church

Surrounded by larch and pine trees,
overlooking the River Dee,
stands CRATHIE *Parish Church,*
commonly known as Crathie Kirk.

Visitors are always welcome to
share Sunday worship.

Crathie Church painted in 1911 by William Smith Junior.
Courtesy of The Mary Evans Picture Library.

Since 1979 Crathie Kirk has been linked with the Church in neighbouring Braemar. The combined Parish covers over 180,000 acres set in some of the most spectacular scenery to be found in the North East of Scotland.

Crathie Kirk is part of the Church of Scotland, the Church established in Scotland by Act of Parliament with the responsibility for the spiritual welfare of the people of Scotland. It dates from the Reformation in 1560 and gradually evolved a system of Presbyterian Government which was written into the Act of Union in 1707. Under this system there is a hierarchy of Church Courts rather than a hierarchy of Bishops.

In a Parish there is a Kirk Session, consisting of the Minister and the ruling Elders who are appointed from the members of the Congregation. This body is responsible for the spiritual oversight of the parish. A group of parishes, each represented by the Minister and an Elder, forms a Presbytery and the supreme court is the General Assembly which meets once a year in Edinburgh. Legends tell of two Celtic missionaries who came to Deeside. The earliest was St Colm who probably came from the Church founded by St Ninian in Whithorn in the 6th Century. He was followed in the 8th Century by St Monire who is said to have baptised converts to Christianity in a pool of the River Dee near Balmoral Castle, still called Polmanire.

There have been several centres of worship in Crathie from the 6th Century. Still visible are the remains of the 14th century Church, dedicated to St Monire within the grounds of the old parish graveyard, situated close by the banks of the River Dee.

The church ruins and the old graveyard can be seen from the front door of the present church. Many of the local people who served Queen Victoria are buried here, including her personal attendant, John Brown. On a number of headstones are personal epitaphs from Queen Victoria. This old church in the graveyard was in use until the latter part of the 18th Century but became too small for the growing population of the parish. A new, simple, unpretentious building typical of Scottish Presbyterian churches of the time was built on the site of the present church in 1805.

Ruins of the 14th century church dedicated to St. Monire

Traditionally the Faith was brought to Crathie by a follower of St. Kentigern, St. Monire, in the 6th century.

It was to this church that Queen Victoria came in 1848 on coming to Balmoral Castle. This began the custom, which continues to this day, of members of the Royal Family and their guests worshipping with local people in the parish church.

Queen Victoria laid the foundation stone of the present church in 1893 and the new church was completed and dedicated in 1895. Funds for the new building were raised by subscription and gifts from parishioners and members of the public. A gift of £2,000 was made by Queen Victoria's daughters Princess Beatrice and Princess Louise who raised the money at a Bazaar held in the grounds of Balmoral Castle.

The church as it appeared in 1882 from The GRAPHIC.
Courtesy of The Mary Evans Picture Library.

A watercolour by William Simpson in 1882 of HM Queen Victoria in her carriage journeying through the Highlands from her house Glass-Alt-Shiel, on the shore of Loch Muick.

Courtesy of The Fine Art Society, London / The Bridgeman Art Library.

The INTERIOR

The interior of the church reflects the history of its long connection with the Royal Family. The beautiful Communion Table and the reredos were the gift of King George V and Queen Mary in memory of Edward VII. The Communion Table is made of white Iona marble with light veining in green and black. The skilful cutting of the three front panels has created a unique cross. The reredos is made from oak which came from a country house in Leicestershire and the fine carving is modelled on that to be found in King's College Chapel in Aberdeen.

The reredos and the Communion table.

The Chancel.

The baptismal font, of polished Kemnay and Rubislaw granite, was the gift of the Queen Victoria's son Arthur, Duke of Connaught and Strathearn.

The font

The lectern was the gift of Rev. Dr Colin Campbell. The small lectern on the Communion Table bears the red, royal-crested Bible given by Her Majesty the Queen in 1962 to mark the 25th year of Dr John Lamb's ministry in Crathie.

As you enter the Church you sense that this is a place of worship and prayer. Looking towards the apse, the pulpit and prayer desk are situated at either side and the Communion Table in the centre, lit by the soft colours of the surrounding stained glass windows. On either side of the Communion Table are the Elders' seats.

The Church is cruciform in shape and is built of a local granite which came from the Inver Quarry on Invercauld Estate. The architect was A. Marshall Mackenzie A.R.S.A. from Aberdeen. The basic style of architecture is Gothic although there are some Norman features. The nave and the north transept seat about 300 people. The choir has a gallery at the west end of the Church in the organ loft. The original organ was replaced by an Allen Digital Computer instrument in 1997.

The lectern, a gift of the Rev. Dr Colin Campbell.

The south transept, the Royal transept, with a separate entrance, is set apart for the use of the Queen, the Royal Family and the Royal Household. The north transept has the pews of the Laird of Invercauld and the Laird of Abergeldie.

On the north wall of the nave are the colours of the local Regiment the First Battalion the Gordon Highlanders which were laid up in the presence of His Royal Highness the Prince of Wales, Colonel-in-Chief of the Regiment, in 1988.

The tower rises above the crossing between the nave and the transepts and has four bells, rung before all services. These were the gift of Princess Beatrice, Queen Victoria's youngest daughter. The bells each have a stirring inscription:

We praise Thee O Lord

I sound and resound to Thee O Lord
To call Thy people to hear Thy Word

There is a God who heareth prayer
Both night and day

O pray to Him,
Pray everywhere and ever pray

Each Sunday morning the worship of God takes place and often the congregation is able to welcome visitors from around the world who come to share in the worship as they enjoy the peace and beauty of this lovely part of Scotland.

A 19th century print of Queen Victoria, Prince Albert and family boarding the Royal Train for Scotland.
Courtesy of The Transport Museum, London. / The Bridgeman Art Library Library .

In the north transept are to be seen the crests of the Scottish Regiments who have served as a Royal Guard when the Court is at Balmoral. They are : The Cameronians, The King's Own Scottish Borderers, The Black Watch, The Royal Scots, The Gordon Highlanders, The Argyll and Sutherland Highlanders and The Queen's Own Highlanders. In the centre of the second row is the crest of the Scottish Division.

Pews of the Lairds of Invercauld and Abergeldie.

The PULPIT

The pulpit, which is of unique design, is hexagonal in form and is made from eighteen different varieties of Scottish granites; Ben Cruachan, Dalmore, Dyce and Rubislaw are some of them. A column of beautiful red granite was the gift of Sir William C. Brookes and came from his estate of Glen Tanar. The Royal Household of Queen Victoria joined in giving the pulpit to the Church which was designed by A. Marshall Mackenzie. Inset to the moulding round the pulpit are marble pebbles which were collected by Queen Victoria's fourth daughter, Princess Louise, Duchess of Argyll on the shores of Iona. The canopy above the pulpit has shields bearing various ecclesiastical symbols.

Princess Louise, Duchess of Argyll after Winterhalter

By courtesy of the Trustees of the 10th Duke of Argyll.

The pulpit.

WINDOWS and FURNISHINGS

T he stained glass is largely Victorian and adds greatly to the beauty of the church.

Within the transept are to be found several Royal memorials. The large window given by Queen Victoria is a memorial to six members of her family, her mother Victoria of Saxe-Coburg, her son Leopold, her son-in law Frederick William, her husband Prince Albert, her daughter Alice and Prince Louis, husband of Alice. The two small lancet windows were given in memory of Prince Henry of Battenberg who married Princess Beatrice and the Duke of Clarence, Queen Victoria's grandson.

Window commemorating Queen Victoria's Diamond jubilee.

Window to Prince Henry
of Battenberg.

Window to the Duke
of Clarence and
Avondale.

Window to Rev.
S.J. Ramsay Sibbals.

The rose window above the organ loft.

The rose window on the west wall of the nave was presented to the Church by descendants of Rev. John McInnes, Minister of Crathie from 1715-1748. Like most of the Church of Scotland ministers during the 1745 rebellion McInnes supported the Hanoverian settlement, but one of the local lairds of Crathie, Francis Farquharson of Monaltrie, was an officer in Prince Charles Edward Stuart's army but was captured at Culloden and taken to London under sentence of death. The story is that McInnes travelled to London in the depths of winter, a considerable journey in those days, to plead for Farquharson's life. He was successful and Farquharson was exiled for about 20 years, his estate being forfeited.

The main window in the north transept commemorates Queen Victoria's Diamond Jubilee as Queen of Great Britain. The small lancet window in the north transept is a memorial to the Rev. S.J.Ramsay Sibbald who was minister of Crathie from 1897-1918.

The lancet windows in the apse were a gift of Captain John Garroway, of Glasgow. They depict in the centre, Our Lord, with St Columba and St Bridget on one side and St Andrew and St Margaret on the other side. The large window in the south transept was the gift of Queen Victoria in affectionate remembrance of the six members of her family who died during her lifetime.

View towards the west door.

The
ROYAL TRANSEPT

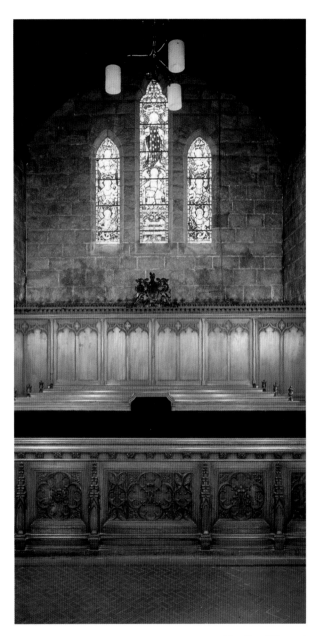

The south transept is set apart for the use of the Sovereign and members of the Royal Family and the Royal Household. The carving on the five oak panels on the front pew depict the Thistle, the Rose and the Shamrock with the Royal and Imperial monogram of Queen Victoria in the centre. These together with the carvings on the Prayer Desk and Elders Stalls were the work of local craftsmen, pupils of the Balmoral School of Arts and Crafts instituted by HRH Prince Albert.

The Duchess of York, later HM Queen Elizabeth The Queen Mother, with her daughters, Princess Margaret Rose and Princess Elizabeth, later HM Queen Elizabeth II and HRH The Duchess of Gloucester arriving for the Crathie Bazaar at Crathie Church Hall.
HULTON GETTY.

The Royal Transept

Detail of prayer desk carving

Plaques to Queen Victoria's eldest daughter Victoria, Empress of Germany and Queen Victoria's second son, the Duke of Edinburgh.

The two white marble medallions were given by King Edward VII in memory of his brother Alfred, Duke of Edinburgh and his sister Victoria, the Princess Royal who became the German Empress, Queen of Prussia and mother of Kaiser William II.

The bust of Queen Victoria was gifted by her son, Edward VII, situated above the foundation stone which she laid. In a cavity within the stone are to be found coins of the realm, a copy of the loyal address read on the occasion of the laying of the stone and other documents relating to the building of the Church. On the facing pillar is a bust of King George V and opposite the pulpit is one of George VI.

Since 1848 when Queen Victoria came first to Balmoral Castle, succeeding sovereigns have regularly worshipped in Crathie Kirk. This tradition has been maintained throughout the years when without formality or ceremonial members of the Royal Family come to share the worship of God with the people of this parish.

Arms of the Gordons of Abergeldie and the Farquharsons of Invercauld.

The bust of King George VI wearing the insignia of the Order of the Thistle.

The bust of Queen Victoria above the foundation stone she laid in 1893.

The bust of King George V wearing the insignia of the Order of the Thistle.

HM Queen Elizabeth II and HRH Prince Philip at Crathie Church.
Courtesy of Aberdeen Journals.

O God, make the doorway of this Church wide enough
to receive all who need human love and fellowship;
Narrow enough to shut out all envy, pride and strife.
Make its threshold smooth enough to be
no stumbling block to children
or barrier to the elderly and disabled.
Let its door be open and inviting to all who enter
And its walls resound with the praise
and worship of your people.

Ministers of Crathie since the Reformation

1563
Sir Laurence Coutts

1567
Richard Christison

1574
John Wilson

1576-1585
Archibald Wilson

1590-1608
David Sanderson

1626-1663
Alexander Ferries (Ferguson) M.A.

1669-1699
William Robertson M.A.

1700-1714
Adam Ferguson M.A.

1715-1748
John McInnes M.A.

1749-1783
Murdoch McLennan

1784-1788
James Wilson M.A.

1789- 1822
Charles McHardy M.A.

1822-1840
Alexander McFarlane

1840-1866
Archibald Anderson M.A.

1867-1873
Malcolm Campbell Taylor D.D.

1874-1896
Archibald Alexander Campbell D.D.

1897-1918
Samuel James Ramsay Sibbald   M.V.O., D.D.

1919-1941
John Stirton C.V.O., D.D.

1937-1963
John Lamb C.V.O., D.D.

1964-1971
Ronald Henderson Gunn Budge
M.V.O., M.A.

1972-1977
Thomas James Trail Nicol
M.V.O., M.B.E., M.C., M.A., D.D.

1979-1995
James Alexander Keith Angus L.V.O.,
T.D., M.A.

1996-
Robert Paterson Sloan M.A., B.D.